Animal Color by Number for kids

THIS COLORING BOOK BELONGS TO

»»»»» Color by number «««««

1 white	**3** orange	**5** green	**7** sky blue
2 yellow	**4** dark red	**6** dark green	**8** blue

Color by number

1 PINK

3 BLUE

2 RED

4 YELLOW

»»»» Color by number ««««

1 white	**4** green	**6** pink	**8** sky blue
2 yellow	**5** dark green	**7** red	**9** blue
3 black			

Color by number

1 YELLOW

3 GREEN

2 ORANGE

4 RED

Color by number

- **1** yellow
- **2** pink
- **3** green
- **4** dark green
- **5** turquoise
- **6** sky blue
- **7** brown
- **8** light gray
- **9** dark gray

Color by number

1 GREEN

3 YELLOW

2 BLACK

4 RED

Color by number

1 white

2 brown

3 green

4 dark green

5 sky blue

6 blue

7 black

»»»» Color by number ««««

1 BLACK

3 PINK

2 BROWN

4 YELLOW

»»»»»» Color by number ««««««

1 white	**3** orange	**5** sky blue	**7** light brown
2 yellow	**4** red	**6** purple	**8** dark brown

»»»» Color by number ««««

1 GREEN	3 YELLOW
2 BROWN	4 RED

Color by number

1 white	**3** yellow	**5** green	**7** brown
2 sky blue	**4** orange	**6** dark green	**8** dark red

»»»» Color by number ««««

1 BLUE

3 BLACK

2 YELLOW

4 PINK

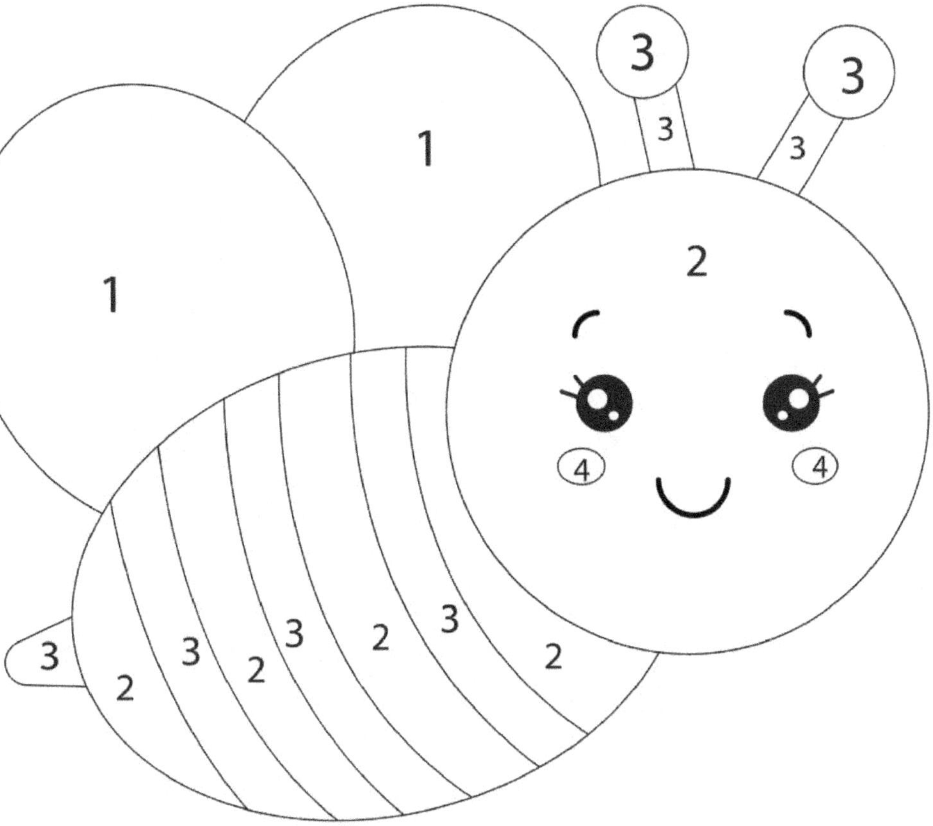

»»»» Color by number ««««

1 white	**3** yellow	**5** sky blue	**7** dark violet
2 light gray	**4** orange	**6** blue	**8** black

»»»»» Color by number «««««

1 ORANGE

3 BROWN

2 RED

Color by number

- **1** white
- **2** yellow
- **3** black
- **4** orange
- **5** red
- **6** sky blue
- **7** blue
- **8** dark violet
- **9** brown

»»»»»» Color by number ««««««

1 BROWN

3 PINK

2 ORANGE

4 BLACK

Color by number

1 yellow	**3** pink	**5** green	**7** blue
2 orange	**4** red	**6** dark green	**8** dark violet

»»»»» Color by number «««««

1 YELLOW

3 RED

2 ORANGE

Color by number

1 white	**4** green	**6** sky blue	**8** light brown
2 yellow	**5** dark green	**7** blue	**9** dark brown
3 red			

»»»» Color by number ««««

1 BROWN

3 BROWN

2 YELLOW

4 PINK

Color by number

1 white	**3** pink	**5** green	**7** sky blue
2 yellow	**4** purple	**6** dark green	**8** blue

Color by number

1 GREEN

3 YELLOW

2 BROWN

4 RED

Color by number

- **1** yellow
- **2** orange
- **3** green
- **4** dark green
- **5** sky blue
- **6** turquoise
- **7** brown

»»»» Color by number ««««

1 ORANGE

3 BLACK

2 BROWN

Color by number

- **1** white
- **2** gray
- **3** pink
- **4** green
- **5** dark green
- **6** turquoise
- **7** sky blue
- **8** blue
- **9** dark violet
- **10** black

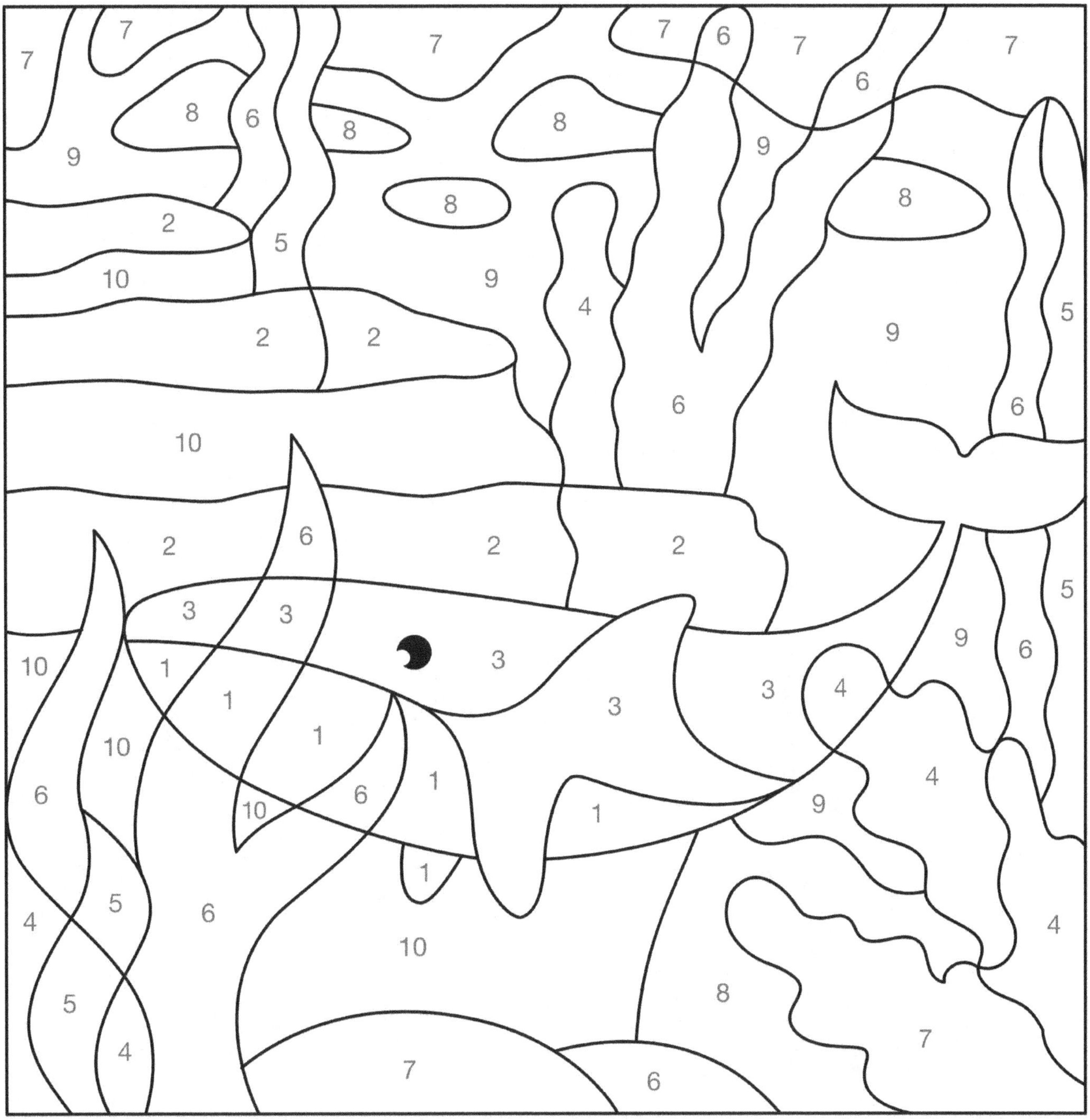

»»»» Color by number ««««

1 BLUE

3 RED

2 PURPLE

»»»»» Color by number «««««

1 white	**4** orange	**7** dark green	**9** blue
2 light gray	**5** red	**8** sky blue	**10** brown
3 yellow	**6** green		

Color by number

1 GRAY

3 RED

2 BLUE

Color by number

1 white	**3** green	**5** turquoise	**7** brown
2 orange	**4** dark green	**6** dark violet	**8** black

»»»»» Color by number «««««

1 BLUE

3 RED

2 PURPLE

Color by number

1 white

2 yellow

3 orange

4 green

5 dark green

6 sky blue

7 blue

Color by number

1 BLUE

3 ORANGE

2 BROWN

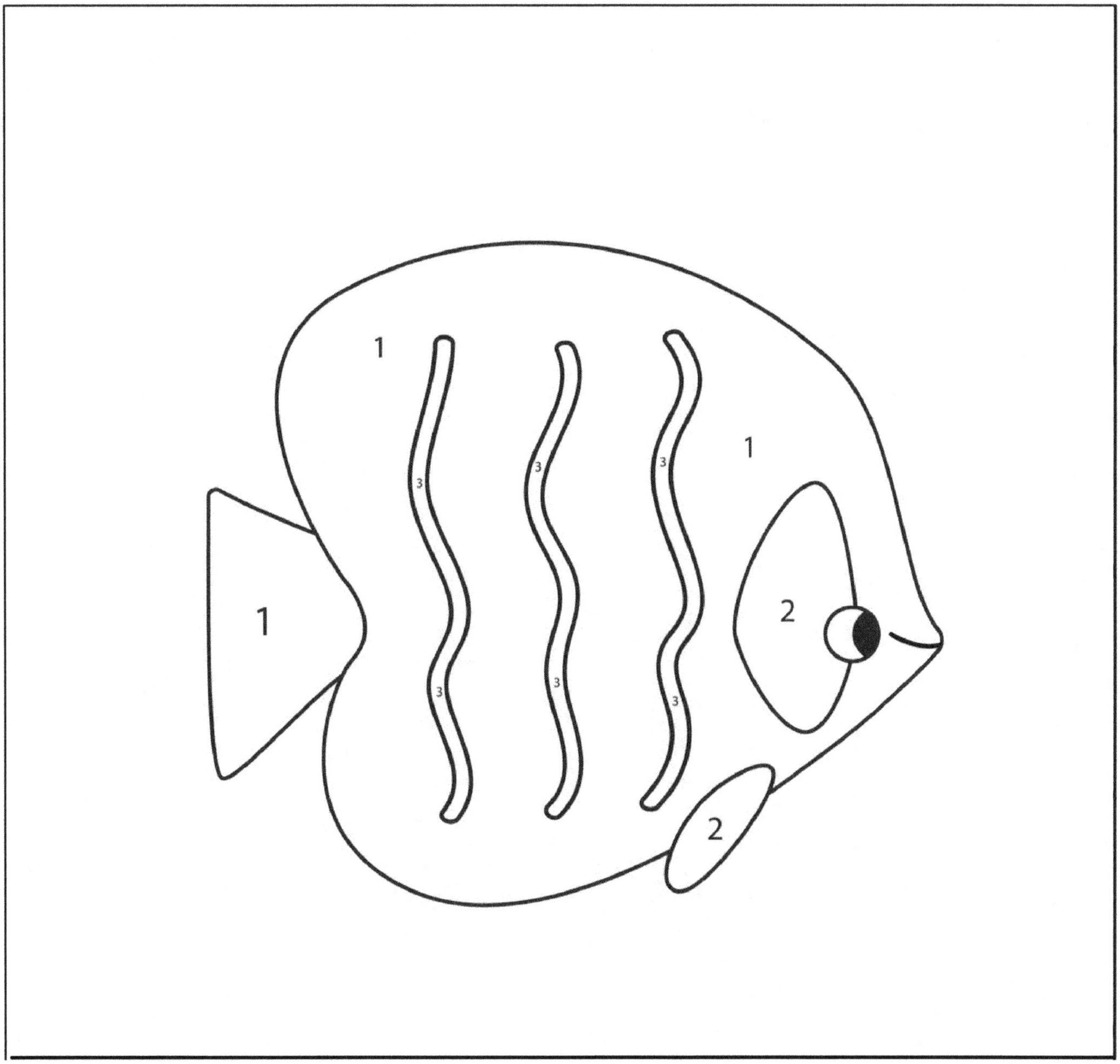

Color by number

1 white	**4** yellow	**6** pink	**8** dark red
2 light gray	**5** orange	**7** red	**9** brown
3 dark gray			

Color by number

1 BROWN

3 ORANGE

2 PINK

4 BLACK

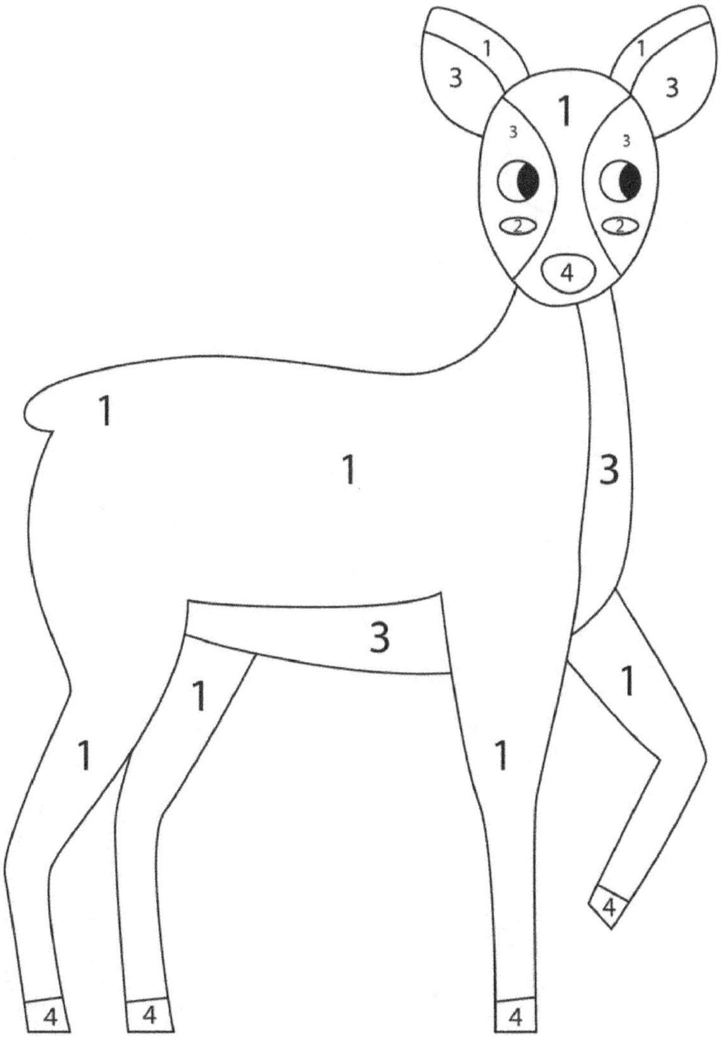

»»»»»» Color by number ««««««

- **1** yellow
- **2** orange
- **3** light brown
- **4** dark brown
- **5** sky blue
- **6** blue
- **7** dark violet
- **8** black

Color by number

1 YELOW	3 BROWN
2 ORANGE	4 PINK

Color by number

- **1** white
- **2** yellow
- **3** orange
- **4** green
- **5** dark green
- **6** sky blue
- **7** blue
- **8** dark violet

»»»» Color by number ««««

1 GREEN

3 ORANGE

5 RED

2 BROWN

4 YELLOW

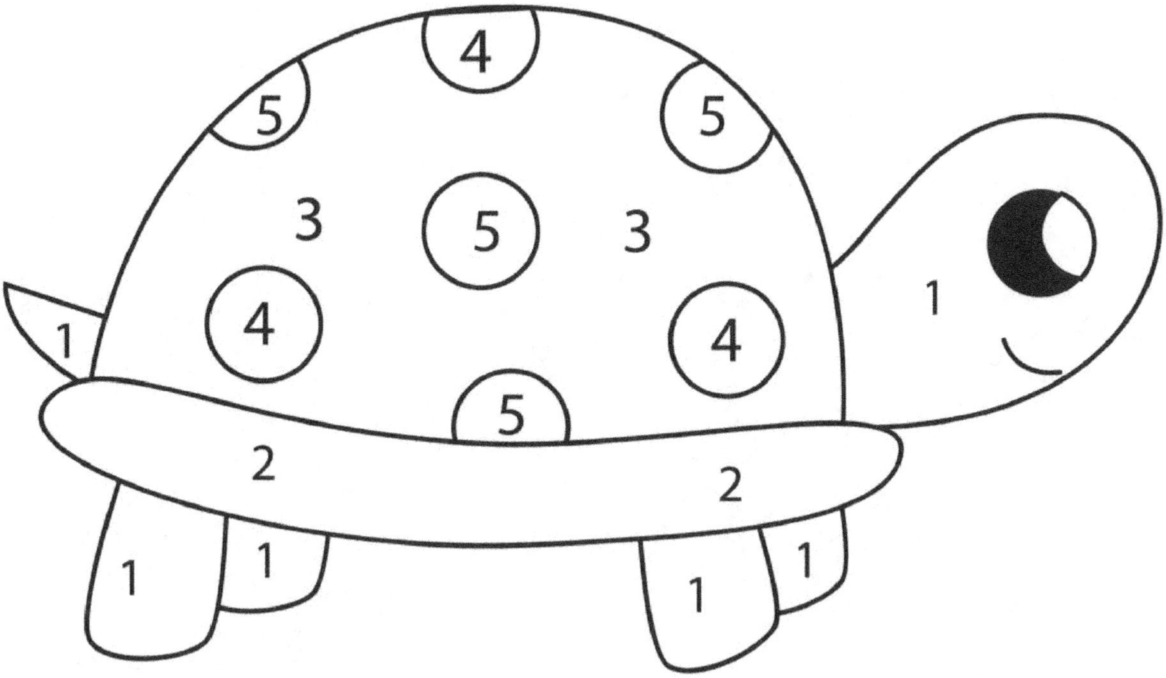

Color by number

- **1** white
- **2** yellow
- **3** orange
- **4** green
- **5** dark green
- **6** sky blue
- **7** blue
- **8** dark violet

Hey there!!!

We hope you enjoyed our book. As a small family company, your feedback is very important to us. Please let us know how you like our book at:

believepublisher@gmail.com

Without your voice we don't exist!

Please, support us and leave a review!

Thank you!!!

www.ingramcontent.com/pod-product-compliance
Lightning Source LLC
LaVergne TN
LVHW060214080526
838202LV00052B/4275
* 9 7 8 4 4 3 9 2 4 0 7 6 3 *